Madonna

Madonna

by Keith Elliot Greenberg

Lerner Publications Company
Minneapolis

Acknowledgements

This book contains information from articles by M. Stanley, Laura Fissinger, Brian Haugh, Cathleen McGuigan, Bill Barol, Jane Briggs-Bunting, Julie Greenwalt, Mary Shaughnessy, Carl Arrington, Denise Worrell, Cathy Booth, John Skow, and Jonathon Gross.

Copyright © 1986 by Lerner Publications Company

LIBRARY OF CONGRESS CATALOGING-IN-PUBLICATION DATA

Greenberg, Keith Elliot.
    Madonna.

    Summary: Describes the life and career of the rock singer and examines her recent appearances in music videos and feature films.
    1. Madonna, 1959-   —Juvenile literature. 2. Rock musicians—United States—Biography—Juvenile literature. [1. Madonna, 1959-   . 2. Musicians. 3. Rock Music] I. Title.
ML3930.M26G7   1986   784.5′4′00924 [B] [92]   85-18030
ISBN 0-8225-1606-3 (lib. bdg.)

Manufactured in the United States of America

2   3   4   5   6   7   8   9   10   96   95   94   93   92   91   90   89   88   87

Contents

The "It" Girl 7

Growing Up 11

New York and Paris 19

Success and Controversy 25

Relaxation 33

The Future 37

The "It" Girl

Since photography was invented, Americans have singled out a special woman every year or two to grace their calendars, their posters, their magazine covers, and their movie screens. Long ago, somebody coined the term "it" girl to describe the woman who was "it" at the moment. British rock star Elvis Costello was referring to the "it" girl when he sang, "You see her picture in a thousand places 'cause she's this year's girl." Betty Grable, Marilyn Monroe, Raquel Welch, Farrah Fawcett, and Cheryl Tiegs have all been "it" girls in the past.

The latest "it" girl is Madonna, a singing sensation with exotic looks and an original style to match her verbal ability. Madonna's much-copied wardrobe consists of lace tights, short tube skirts, mesh stockings, midriffs, gauzy shirts, rubber bracelets and lace gloves. She knows how to look glamorous and casual at the same time. Tying big, floppy rags in her frosted hair and hanging large crosses from her neck and ears, Madonna is considered by some people to be the Marilyn Monroe of the 1980s. Fashion photographer Francesco Scavullo called her "Baby Dietrich," comparing the entertainer with Marlene Dietrich, the beautiful and stormy German movie actress of the 1930s and 1940s.

Can the Madonna phenomenon be explained? *Time* magazine didn't think so. "Big time show biz is three-fourths mass hysteria, especially when teenagers and rock music are involved, and anyone who thinks he can explain it fully is dreaming," stated the magazine. Many people, however, claim they can, at least partially, explain Madonna's popularity. Some say that Madonna's image is that of the girl "you hate to love," one who is irresistible even though you know she will break your heart. Indeed, Madonna admits to ensnaring new fans into her web by "flirting" with them through her records and videos. "Bruce Springsteen was born to run," she said. "I was born to flirt."

That comment, of course, was meant as a joke. Madonna has a great sense of humor, and that is another reason for her popularity. In her videos, she finds subjects which people have taken seriously for so long, like love and money, and does comical spoofs of them. Her quality of laughing at the world and laughing at herself helps bring out the child in all of us. Everyone can relate to the singer when, at the end of her show, a male voice booms over the loudspeaker, "Madonna, get off that stage this instant!" Madonna whines back, "Daddy, do I have to?"

But she's also hard-headed when she has to be. "I'm tough, ambitious and I know exactly what I want," she said, and those who know her agree. Perhaps that is another reason why America is worshipping Madonna. With her unconventional manner, strong will, and creative way of getting a point across, she is truly an American success story.

Growing Up

Madonna Louise Veronica Ciccone was born August 16, 1959, while her parents were visiting her maternal grandparents in Bay City, Michigan. Her father was the son of Italian immigrants and had grown up in an industrial town in Pennsylvania. He majored in engineering in college and then moved to Michigan to take a job in the automotive industry. Because he had been poor when he was growing up, he instilled in his children a desire to get the most out of their lives. He believed in teaching by example: if he told his kids not to do something, he was careful not to do it either.

Madonna's mother was of French-Canadian ancestry. Relatives still say that Madonna has many of her mother's features. The singer recalls that her mother was a "very forgiving, angelic person." When the children didn't behave, they were never hit. Instead, Mr. and Mrs. Ciccone would hug them and speak to them quietly.

When Madonna was six, her mother died of breast cancer. Madonna watched the woman grow weaker and weaker. Once, when her daughter asked her to get off the couch and play, Mrs. Ciccone was too weak to comply. "I remember feeling stronger than she was," Madonna said. "I was so little and I put my arms around her and I could feel her body underneath me sobbing and I felt like she was the child.... That was the turning point.... I think that made me grow up fast. I knew I could either be sad and weak and not in control or I could take control and say it's going to get better."

After her mother died, Madonna's father hired numerous housekeepers to help take care of his children. He eventually married one housekeeper and had children with her. From his two marriages combined, he had eight children.

With so many brothers and sisters, Madonna had to speak out in order to get what she wanted. "It's easy for me to come out and say stuff," she said. "I think I really developed that aspect of my personality growing up in my family....feeling like I had to defend myself."

Madonna still plays dress-up on stage. Her costume for "Like A Virgin" in concert is a bare-midriff wedding dress.

Because she was the oldest girl in the family, Madonna had more responsibilities than the other children. She began to look at herself as a sort of Cinderella, with a stepmother who kept her working around the house.

Madonna's stepmother bought all the girls in the family the same dresses, so the future singer had to go to great pains to stand out. She bought oddly colored knee socks and put strange bows in her hair. Her Catholic school required that students wear uniforms. To appear different from the others, Madonna would "put bright panty bloomers underneath and hang upside down on the monkey bars at recess."

Still, in spite of her outrageousness, the girl became friends with several of her nuns and even considered becoming one. She thought nuns were beautiful, pure, and disciplined. They seemed very serene to her. Madonna also liked some of their values, particularly those stressing fair treatment for all, and condemning stealing, cheating, and lying.

No doubt, the nuns who taught Madonna never realized that the crucifixes they wore around their necks would not only influence the fashion tastes of their young student, but would also one day influence the fashion tastes of an entire nation. Madonna loved the way the large crosses looked around the nuns' necks, and she began including them in her wardrobe.

At home, all the children in Madonna's family had to learn to play a musical instrument. Madonna began taking piano lessons, but didn't like them and convinced her father to register her for ballet, jazz, tap, and baton twirling lessons. She began acting in school plays and dreaming about life as a star. Her idols at the time were bombshell actresses like Carole Lombard, Judy Holliday, and Marilyn Monroe, and soulful singers like Nancy Sinatra, Eartha Kitt, Martha Reeves, Diana Ross, the Chrystals, and the Shirelles. Her black girlfriends introduced her to the spirited "Motown sound," and she happily remembers listening to black music at backyard dances.

In high school, Madonna was a cheerleader, before she decided to concentrate on dancing full-time. Her instructor, Christopher Flynn, would become one of the biggest influences in her life. He told her that she had a magical, starlike quality. Her face, he said, had the beauty of a Roman statue. She was stunned. She had never thought of herself as beautiful. Flynn claimed that her charm was internal rather than superficial.

Today, Flynn remembers Madonna as being "one of the best students I ever had, a very worldly sort of woman even as a child."

Madonna's unique style of dressing developed during this period. She lived in the tights and leotards she wore for dancing, but made them uniquely hers by adding patterns of tears and runs. One day, when she couldn't find anything to hold her long hair in place, she chose an old pair of tights.

Madonna launched her career as an actress in the movie *Desperately Seeking Susan.* She designed her own costumes for the role of Susan, and her style came through from floppy bows to high-heeled boots.

16

The tights were eventually replaced by large bows. Within a few short years, girls around the country would be tying their hair a certain way because of Madonna's quick decision in a dance studio that day.

New York
and
Paris

After three semesters in the University of Michigan's dance program, Madonna chose to leave school and realize a lifelong dream by moving to New York City. She arrived in 1978 with a suitcase full of dance clothes and $35 in her pocket. Under her arm was a large baby doll, which she brought along to keep her company during the many lonely nights ahead. In her own words, she moved "from one dive to the next" and lived on popcorn. "I still love it," she said. "Popcorn is cheap and it fills you up."

Her talents were recognized by the prestigious Alvin Ailey dance school, which gave her a scholarship. She supported herself by working at the school and at Dunkin' Donuts.

The life of luxury that would be at her fingertips later was still miles away. When her father visited her in New York, he was "mortified." Madonna said, "He couldn't understand how I could live in a roach-infested building with winos in the hallways....He thought I was in a rathole."

Madonna wanted to work with the top dance companies, which she found to be already well-stocked with performers. Rather than "hang around for five years" until a position opened, she started going to musical-theater auditions. She learned that Christopher Flynn was not the only person to recognize her star quality.

At one audition, she caught the eye of a member of a management company. They were already managing French disco singer Patrick Hernandez, whose tune, *Born to Be Alive*, was then a hit. The management company convinced Madonna to move to Paris, where they promised to make her famous. Unfortunately, they did not know *how* to make her famous.

"They promised me everything," Madonna said. "'You'll live like a queen,' they said. 'We'll give you a vocal coach, you'll decide what direction you want to go in.' It was the only time I lived comfortably in my life, but I missed struggling with my friends."

Madonna knew that for her the only road to stardom was hard work. "Madonna only wanted one thing — to be a star," said Mrs. Jean Claude Pallerin, who knew the singer in Paris. "And when she left Paris, she promised that she would come back a star."

Back in New York, Madonna moved into an abandoned synagogue with her friends Dan and Ed Gilroy, now part of the rock group Breakfast Club. She wrote music with them and they taught her guitar licks. She describes this period of her life as her "intensive musical training."

Next came a female manager who encouraged Madonna to keep writing music. The problem was that "we didn't see eye-to-eye on the direction I was headed. She wanted to do Pat Benatar-like rock. I was trying for a more funky sound, black stuff. She told me I couldn't do that because I was a little white girl. I refused to listen."

Madonna dropped her manager and decided to make a tape of "music that I would dance to." She planned to use this tape as her introduction to record companies. Steve Bray, a musician Madonna knew from the University of Michigan, had keys to many New York studios. "We'd sneak into them late at night to work on the songs and the tape," she said. "Between the two of us, we played enough instruments to do the tape all by ourselves."

Never one to let shyness stand in the way of success, Madonna gave the tape to Mark Kamins, a disc jockey at the New York dance club Danceteria, and would shake in front of his booth while he played her songs. The regulars at the club began to request Madonna's tape, and Kamins thought that his friends at Sire Records would be interested in it. Sire president Seymour Stein had recently taken ill and was in the hospital at the time. "I got this call from my assistant about a Madonna tape that Mark brought," he said. "I arranged for her to meet me at the hospital; then I shaved and had someone bring me a bathrobe from home. When she walked into the room, she filled it with her exuberance and determination. It hit me right away. I could tell she had the drive

Madonna's determination to become a star has impressed everyone who has worked with her. Her inner strength comes through in her stage performances.

to match her talent."

Within months, countless others would make that observation.

Success
and Controversy

Madonna's first album, *Madonna*, was released in July, 1983. A perfectionist, the performer chose an accomplished producer to work on the record instead of her disc jockey friends. Reggie Lucas had produced such artists as Stephanie Mills and Phyllis Hyman, and Madonna was confident that he could help her album hit the top of the charts. For the first few months following its release, however, the record stayed off most major radio stations. Eventually, her song "Borderline" received airplay and climbed into the Top Ten. Her second hit was "Lucky Star."

The singer tried to keep as much control over her material as possible. It was important to her to help conceive her videos. She realized that video was almost as important to a potential superstar as a good-sounding record. Before she toured a certain area, she said, video would acquaint fans there with her style. "It takes the place of touring," she said. "Everybody sees [videos] everywhere."

Madonna established herself as a video queen during the opening moments of "Lucky Star" when she lowered her dark glasses and stared directly at her viewers. The same video made midriffs fashionable again — and Madonna's belly button a much talked-about item.

Her second video, "Borderline," opened up with Madonna break-dancing in slow-motion on the streets of downtown Los Angeles. Her dance partner was ex-boyfriend and disc jockey, John "Jelly Bean" Benitez, who has since become so popular that a film on his life is in the works.

Madonna needed a personal manager, and she wanted the best. She decided to pick Freddy DeMann, who had managed Michael Jackson. DeMann's memory of his first meeting with Madonna is typical: "She had that special magic that very few stars have," he said.

If Madonna's first album hadn't sent shock waves through the music world, then her next record, produced by veteran Nile Rodgers, was guaranteed to do the job.

Madonna out on the town with Jelly Bean Benitez, her dance partner in the "Borderline" video, and also her boyfriend for a time.

The *Like a Virgin* album cover showed Madonna in lace, looking flirtatiously at the camera. Critics blasted the photo — and the video of the album's title track — as being too sexy. Some said that the "Like a Virgin" video was bad for women who want to be seen as more than just a pretty face. Madonna responded that she was very aware of the problems ambitious women face, and she pointed out that the director of "Like a Virgin," Mary Lambert, was a woman.

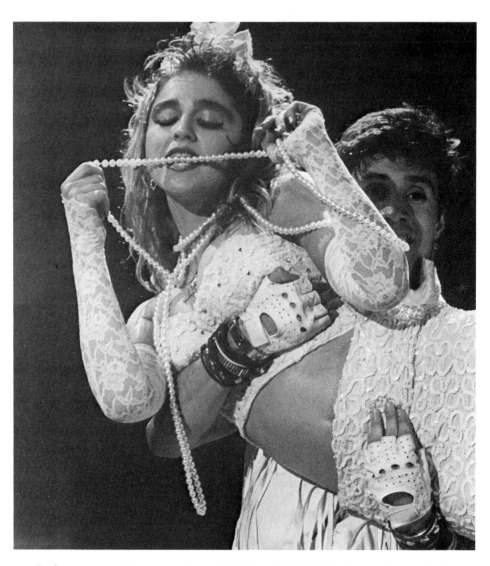

In her concert tour version of "Material Girl," Madonna is carried onstage in a lavish evening gown, swinging ropes of pearls. At the end the male dancers pull out handfuls of "Madonna dollars."

Actually, the theme of "Like a Virgin" is very innocent. True love, Madonna sings, can make a girl feel "shiny and new."

A furor was raised over the video of another song on the *Like a Virgin* album, "Material Girl." In "Material Girl" Madonna, wearing a long, pink evening dress, is showered with pearls and jewelry by a circle of tuxedoed gentlemen. Many felt that the message of the song was that only men with money are worth a girl's while. Madonna countered that "Material Girl" pokes fun at precisely those who have such values. "Look at my video," she said. "The guy who gets me in the end is the sensitive guy with no money."

Madonna's knack for controversy only seems to fuel her popularity. Her first album, *Madonna*, has sold over 2.8 million copies in the United States. *Like a Virgin* has sold 4.5 million copies in America and 2.5 million in other countries. Over 6 million Americans have bought Madonna's singles, and that number is increasing every day.

Having already discovered her success as a recording artist, Madonna has begun making films. She plays a barroom singer in *Vision Quest*. "Crazy For You," the song she sings in the movie, is one of the most requested tunes on American radio stations. She landed a starring role in *Desperately Seeking Susan*, playing a character not unlike herself. "She's this really crazy, lively, wild girl who kind of wreaks havoc in everyone's life," Madonna explained. "I can relate to that. She drifts in and

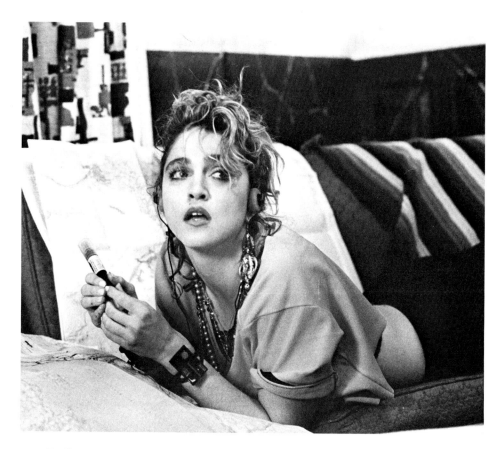

In *Desperately Seeking Susan* **Madonna plays a wild, free character — similar to herself. A fellow actress says that Madonna "had a very clear vision of her character, which other people didn't always have."**

out of guys' lives and they fall in love with her and she says 'later' and stuff like that. The difference is she was kind of a drifter and I am very focused."

Director Susan Seidelman said that Madonna was, at

all times, a total professional on the set. No matter how late she had been working the night before, she was always ready to act as early as the director dictated. Seidelman said that when Madonna first auditioned for the part, she had yet to become a superstar. Until they met her, executives at Orion Pictures had been hesitant to use her.

Once again, that special, starlike quality came shining through.

Relaxation

It is difficult for Madonna to relax. She feels most comfortable working on her songs, her videos, and her movies. "I'm here. I'm there. I love to work," she said. "I guess you'd say I'm a hyperactive adult."

During her free time, the singer enjoys partying with friends. Fellow superstar Prince is sometimes a companion. Madonna attended one of his concerts in Los Angeles a short time back, then joined him on stage for a duet. Later that night, she attended a party at his hotel and was seen around town with him for the next several days, eating in Japanese restaurants and dancing in discos.

When Madonna parties, she stays away from drugs. She doesn't see the point of taking them. "All the feelings I think drugs are supposed to produce in you, confidence or energy, I can produce naturally in my body," she said.

In spite of the words of her song, Madonna is anything but a material girl. "If someone says, 'You're getting a half-million [dollars],' I go, 'Big deal, I don't care,'" she said. "I'm not interested as long as I have enough money to pay the rent and buy all my rubber bracelets and stuff." The two possessions she has to show for her success are a television set and a ten-speed bicycle. "I always said I wanted to be famous. I never *said* I wanted to be rich," she told *People* magazine.

Before going on her 28-city *Virgin* tour, Madonna took a driver's education class and got her license. "I rented a car and it was a thrill," she said.

To keep her 5-foot, 4-inch, 118-pound body in shape, Madonna works out religiously. When she was making *Desperately Seeking Susan,* she would go to the health club at 4:30 A.M. before filming started.

Madonna also loves to read. Her favorite authors include William Faulkner, Ernest Hemingway, and J.D. Salinger. But she admits that she takes pleasure in reading newspapers with lots of juicy celebrity gossip. These

34

days it's easy to understand why: Madonna's name is usually in the headlines of these publications.

The Future

If Madonna's fans can be sure of anything, it's that their idol does not intend to sit on her fame and decrease her work load. She still has too much creativity bursting out of her. If she lives up to her past reputation, that creativity will be released in ways which will rattle the entertainment industry.

Movies are near the top of her priority list. She plans to do a film "loosely based on my life but not exactly.... It'll incorporate all my talents. I'm going to dance in it and sing in it." She feels that performing in front of the cameras is similar to singing a song. "I think that when you are singing a song....it's almost like crying in front of people. Acting is about that too — communicating and being honest....It's just a different way of doing it." One day, she intends to direct a movie. She promises that all her film projects will have a touch of her special sense of humor.

Love will continue to be a theme in her music. However, the future may see Madonna taking this subject a little more seriously. She said that the idea she wants to convey in one of her next songs is: "Love makes the world go 'round."

Her husband, actor Sean Penn, will surely offer Madonna a great deal of inspiration. The couple met while the singer was taping her "Material Girl" video, and friends say their personalities are perfectly matched. Madonna's liveliness is nicely balanced by her husband's shyness.

Their wedding, at a tree-lined estate on the hills above Malibu Beach, was the media event of the summer of 1985. Photographers waited outside the gates to snap pictures of the numerous celebrities who attended, while other gawkers actually rented helicopters to look down on the ceremony.

Madonna looks forward to motherhood. For the moment, however, she is too busy plotting her career to concern herself with settling down. She still has many critics and she wants to show them that she is someone to be taken seriously.

Madonna made her second movie with her new husband. She co-starred with Sean in *Shanghai Surprise*, released in 1986. The critics and the audiences didn't care much for *Shanghai*. But Madonna wasn't fazed. Her 1986 album, *True Blue*, received plenty of good reviews. With this album, critics began to take her music seriously, and several singles from the album were hot on the charts. Madonna's new, beautiful image in her videos and the movie also helped silence critics who said she was all gimmick.

And although she has accomplished more than most people dream about, Madonna has yet to realize her ultimate goal. What might that goal be? "It's the same goal I've always had," she said half-jokingly. "I made it as a little girl. I want to rule the world."

Photo Credits

Orion Pictures, pp. 1, 15, 30
Paul Natkin/Starfile Photo Agency, p. 2
Gary Gershoff/Retna Ltd., pp. 6, 36
John Bellissimo/Retna Ltd., p. 10
Nancy Barr, pp. 13, 28
Bob Gruen/Starfile Photo Agency, p. 18
Danny Chin/Starfile Photo Agency, p. 22
Kevin Mazur/Retna Ltd., pp. 24, 32, 40
Robin Kaplan/Retna Ltd., p. 27

Front cover photo by Michael Putland/Retna Ltd.
Back cover photo by Danny Chin/Starfile Photo Agency